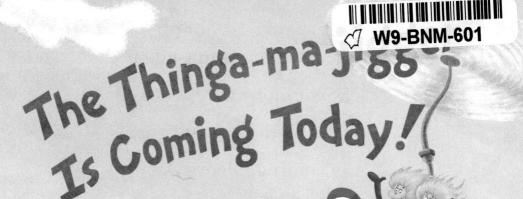

The Thinga-ma-jigger Is Coming Today!

by Tish Rabe
illustrated by
Christopher Moroney

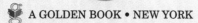

A GOLDEN BOOK • NEW YORK

Seussville.com   pbskids.org/catinthehat   treehousetv.com
Library of Congress Control Number: 2009928183
ISBN: 978-0-375-85927-4
Printed in the United States of America   10 9 8 7

The Thinga-ma-jigger
is coming today!
The Thinga-ma-jigger
is coming. Hooray!

Who's driving this thing?
Is it someone you know?
It's the Cat in the Hat
and he's ready to go!

"Hop on!" calls the Cat.
"I am waiting for you!
With Sally and Nick and
Thing One and Thing Two!"

Flick the Jiggermawhizzer
and we will start zinging
and binging and banging
and ring-a-ding-dinging!

We'll soar to the shores
of Lake Wicki Washoo.

Then fly through the forests
of Jigamaroo!
(Your mother will not
mind at all if you do.)

Press the Shrinkamadoodle!

And we'll get so small . . .

. . . we can dance with the bees
with no problem at all!

We'll glide into a garden
and slide inside flowers.

Then bounce on their petals
for hours and hours!

We'll dive into the ocean.
We'll splash and we'll splish
and study a school
of black angelfish!

Press the Bigamaboodle
and we will get BIGGER!

Here comes the world's
biggest Thinga-ma-jigger!

We'll swoop down a mountain.

Then blast into space.

We'll go zipping and zapping

all over the place!

"I can fly upside down!
I can flip it or flop it.
But I have one question—
just HOW do I stop it?

The Stoppermatoggle
is busted, so how
can I stop this contraption?
Please tell me NOW!"

"Don't worry!" cries Nick.

"I know just what to do.

This is a job for

Thing One and Thing Two!"

So . . .

the Things toot a big toot!

And their big toot is heard . . .

. . . by a faraway, half-asleep
Great Bustard Bird.

The Great Bustard Bird
shows up on the double
and sees that the Cat in the Hat
is in trouble!

The Great Bustard Bird
is quite up to the test.
Stopping Thinga-ma-jiggers
is what he does best!

He comes singing and winging.

For him it's not hard.

He lands the thing safely . . .

. . . in Sally's backyard.

So keep your eyes set
on the big, bright blue sky.
You might see the Thinga-ma-jigger
fly by.

Because some early morning
or late afternoon,
the Thinga-ma-jigger . . .

. . . will be along soon!